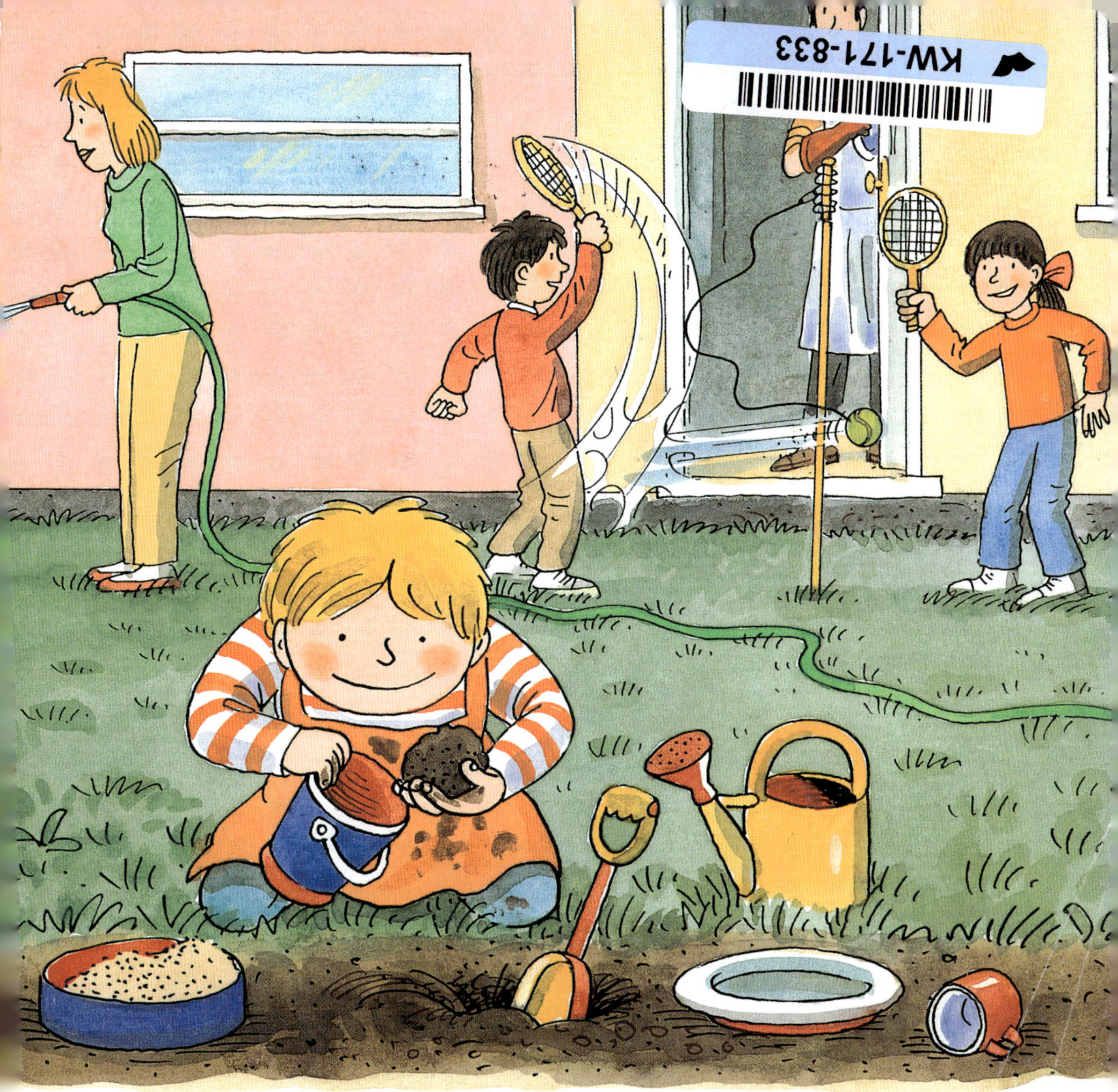

This is mud in my hand.

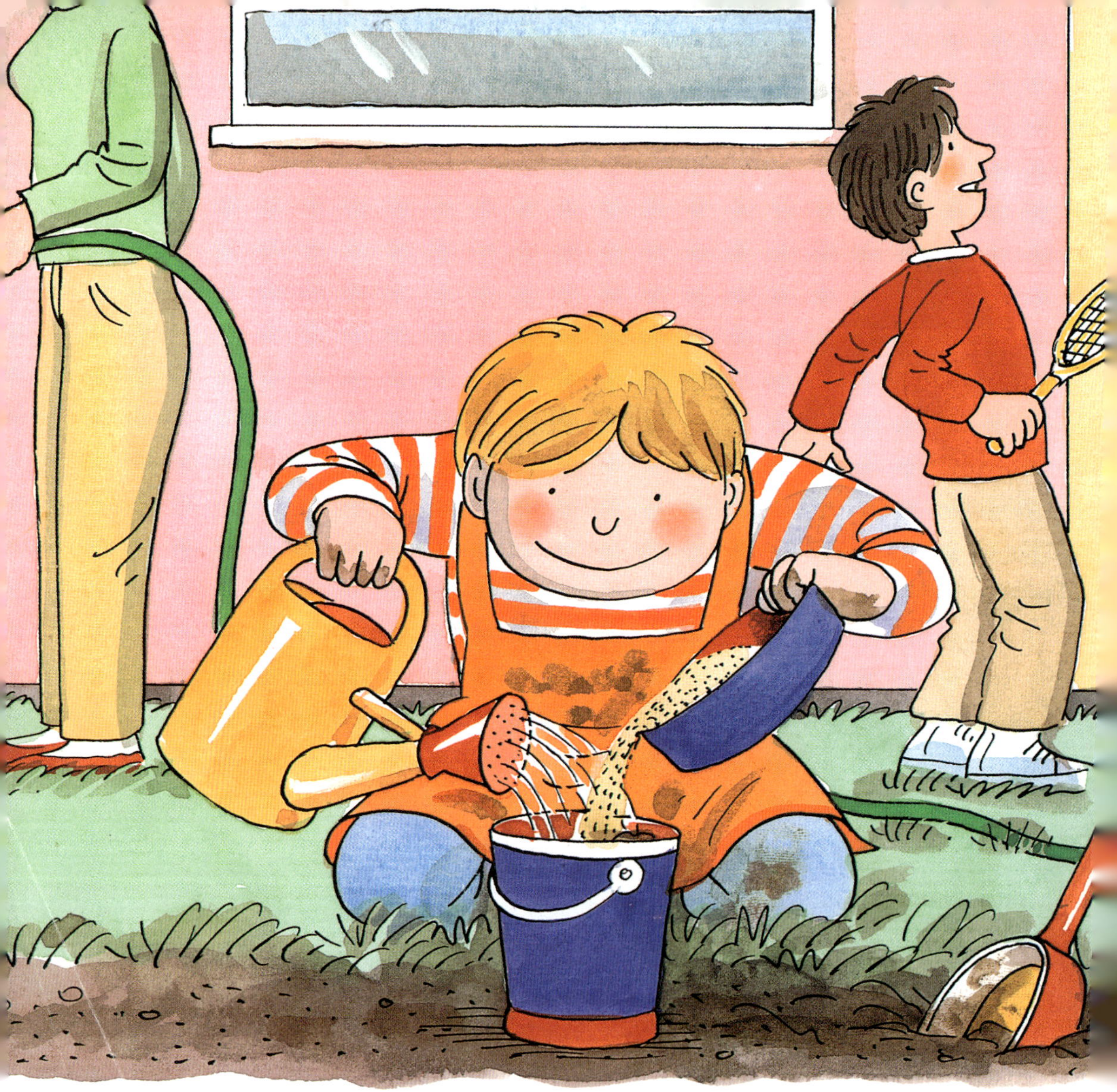

Put in water.

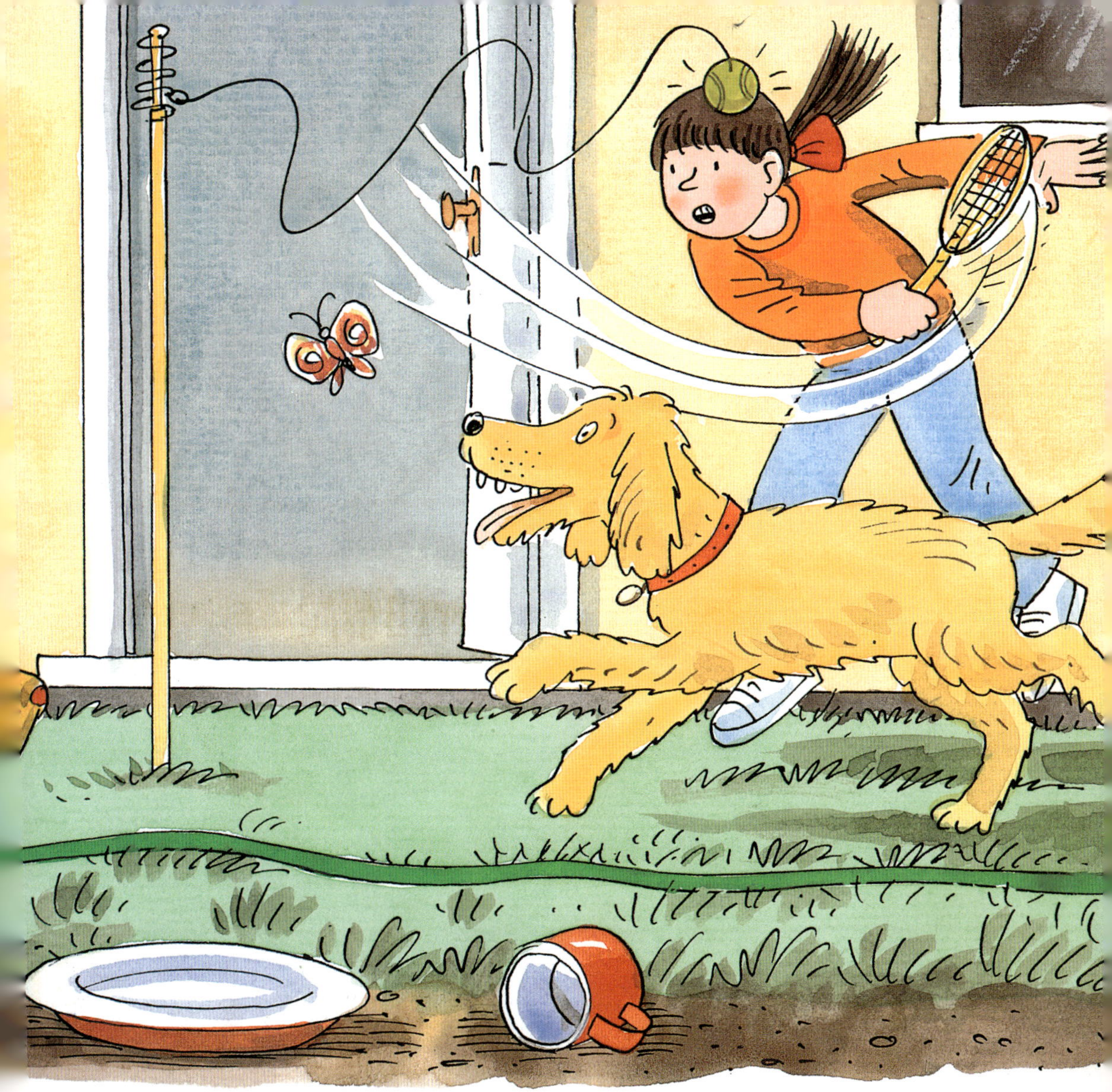

Mix in sand.

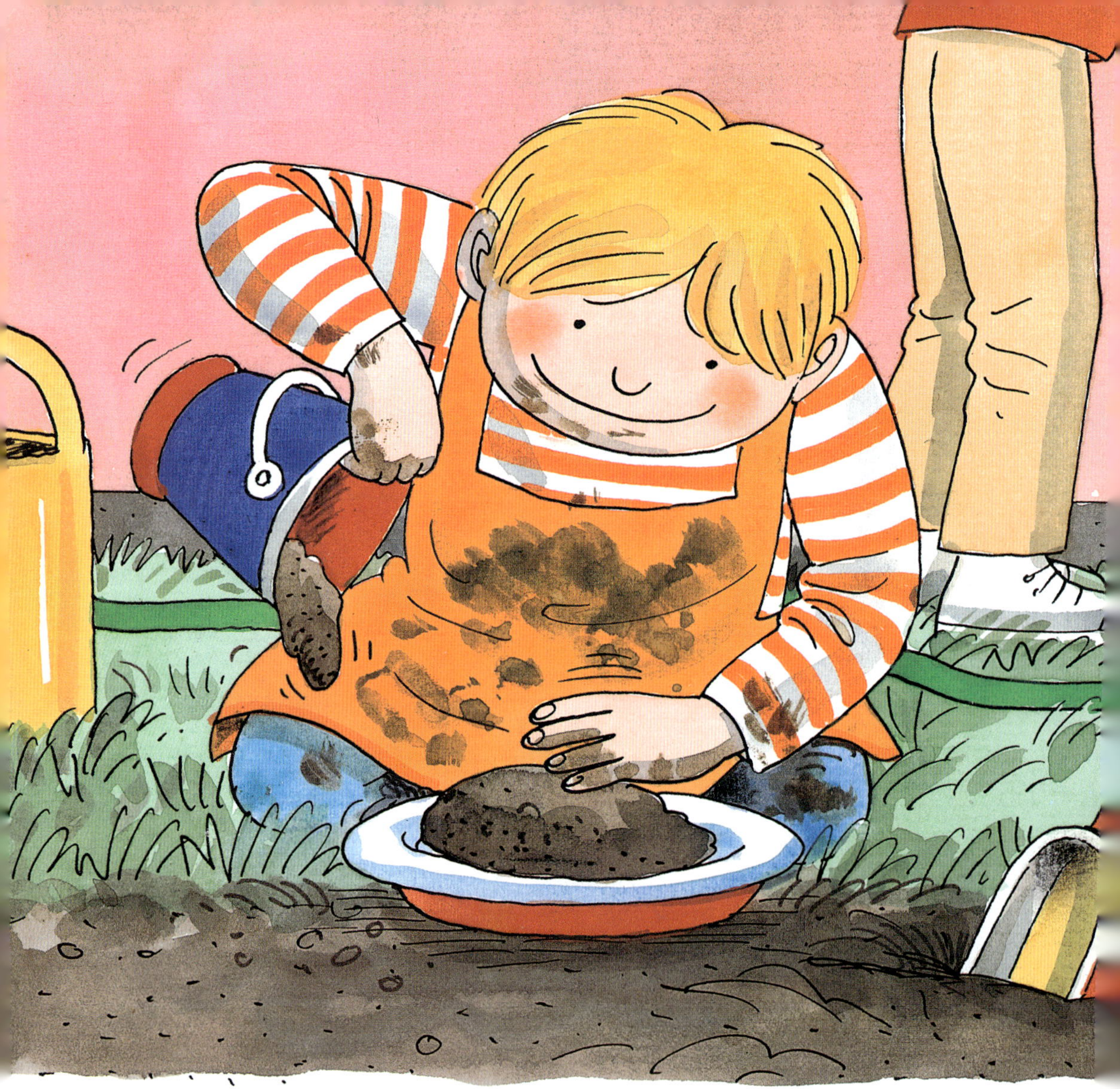

Tip it out.

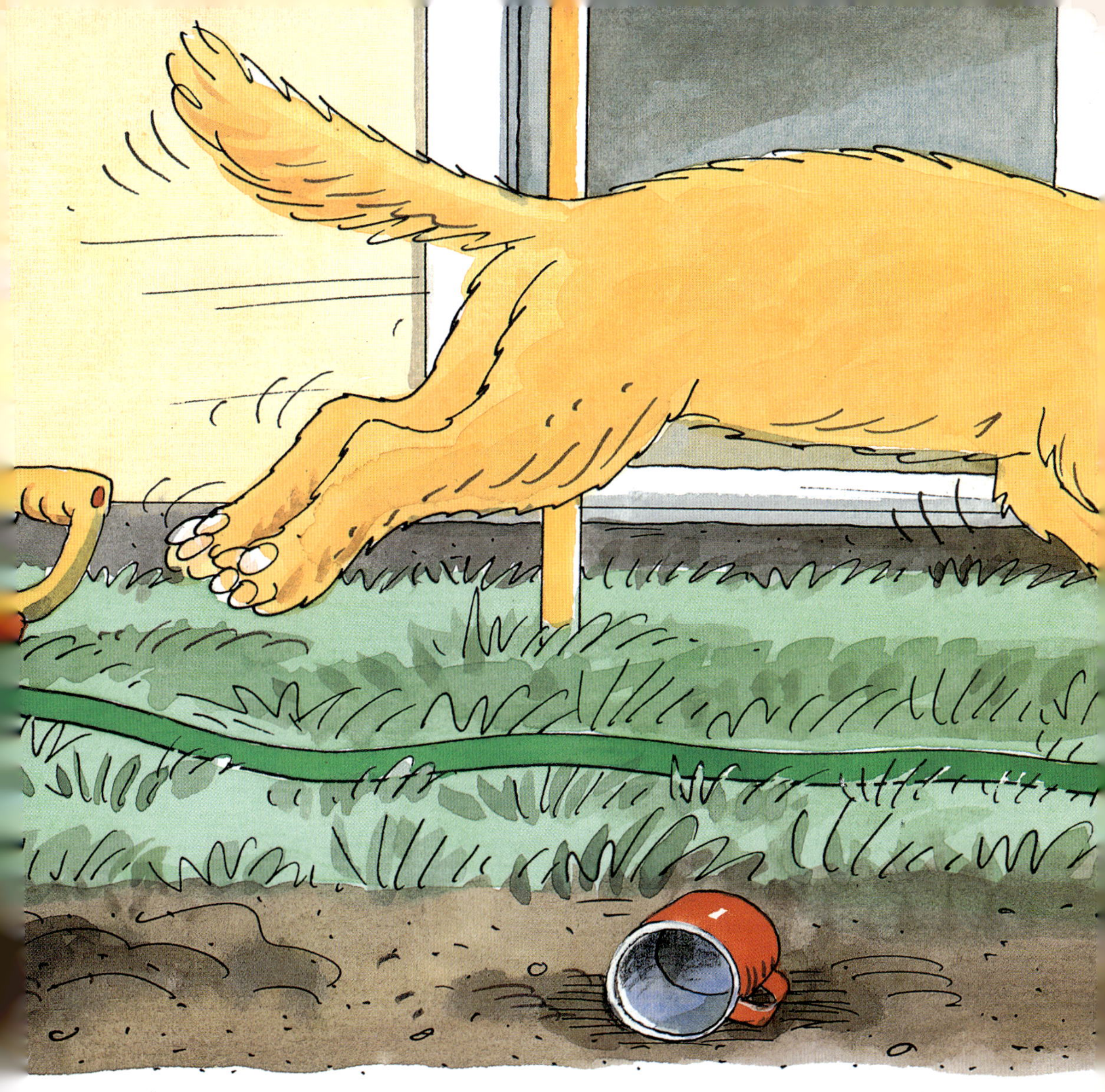

Pat it flat.

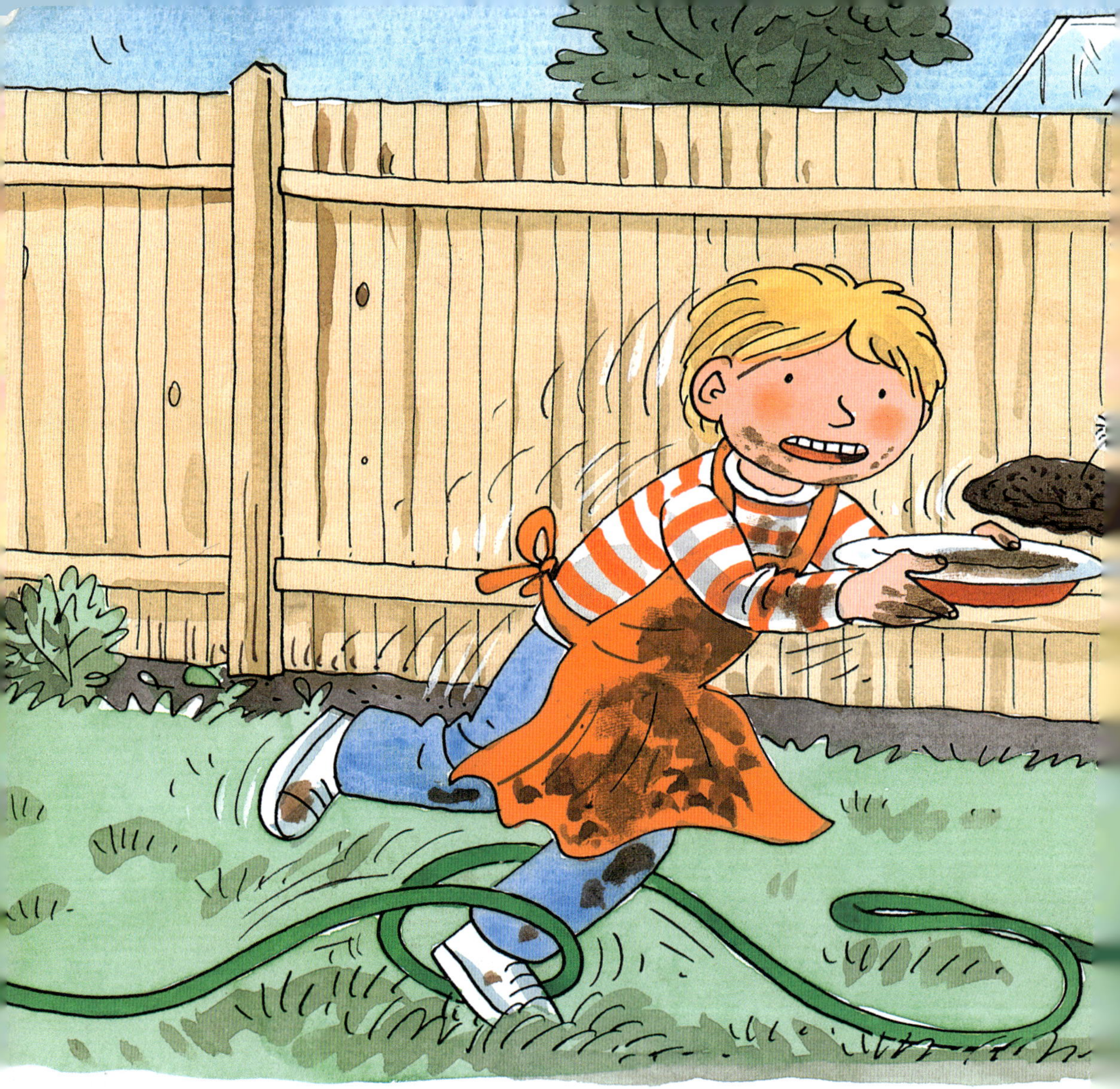

This is a mud pie …

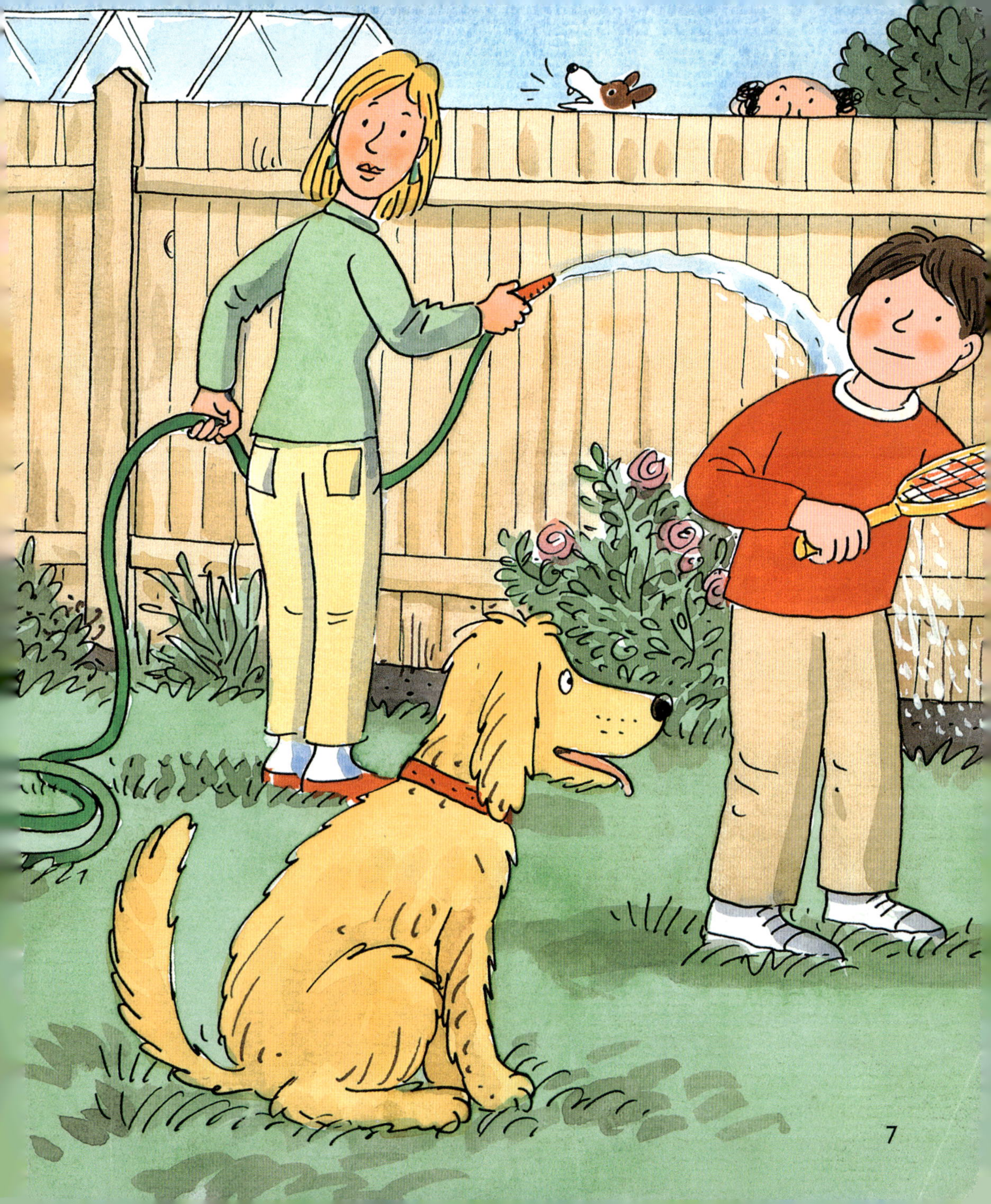

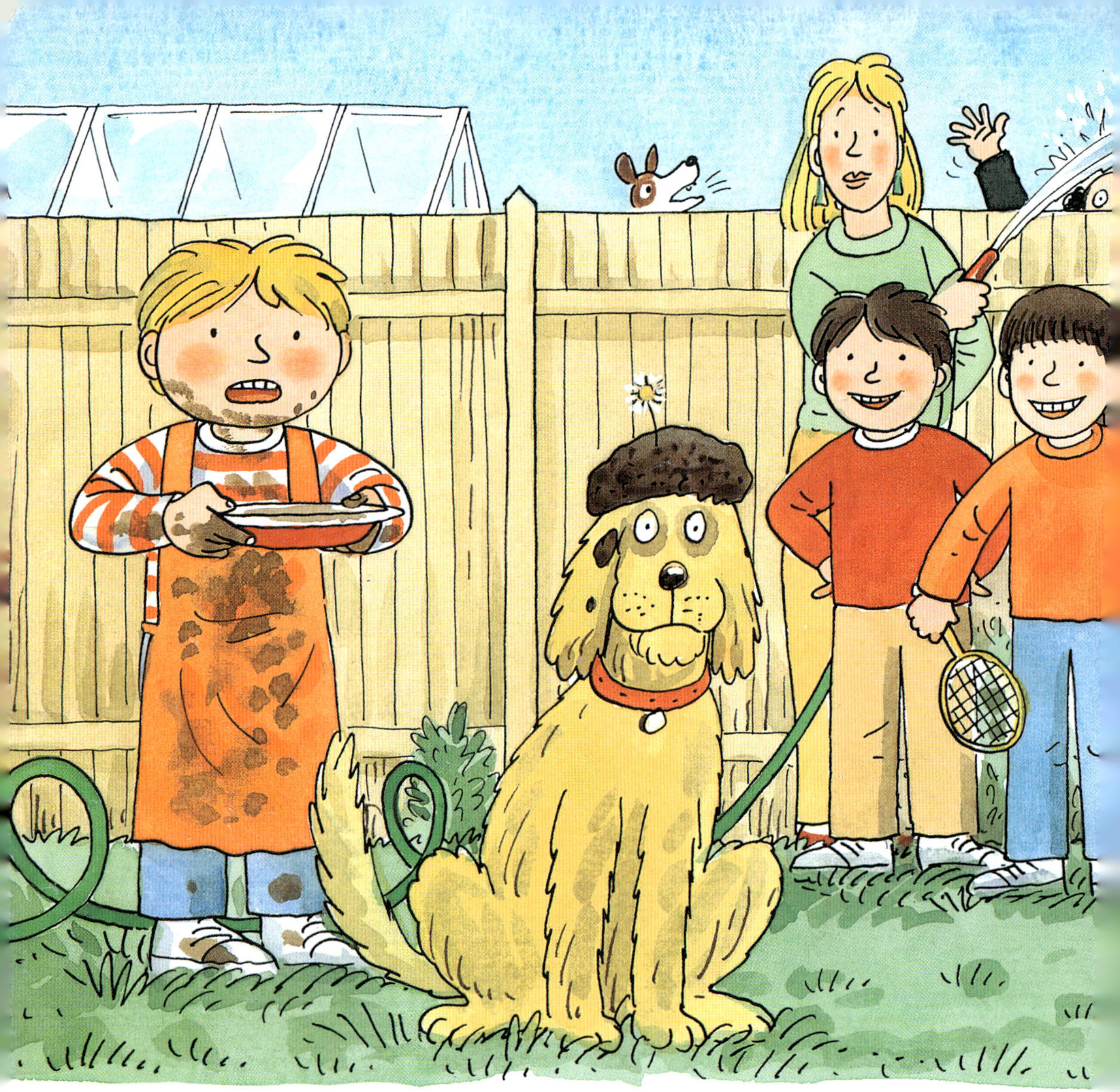

... not a hat.